The Word Wizard's Book of PREFIXES and SUFFIXES

Robin Johnson

Crabtree
Publishing
Company

www.crabtreebooks.com

Word Wizard

Author
Robin Johnson

Publishing plan research and development
Reagan Miller

Editorial director
Kathy Middleton

Project coordinator
Kelly Spence

Editor
Anastasia Suen

Proofreader and indexer
Wendy Scavuzzo

Photo research
Robin Johnson, Katherine Berti

Design & prepress
Katherine Berti

Print coordinator
Katherine Berti

Photographs
All images from Shutterstock

Library and Archives Canada Cataloguing in Publication

Johnson, Robin (Robin R.), author
     The word wizard's book of prefixes and suffixes / Robin Johnson.

(Word wizard)
Includes index.
Issued in print and electronic formats.
ISBN 978-0-7787-1921-2 (bound).--ISBN 978-0-7787-1925-0 (pbk.).--
ISBN 978-1-4271-7793-3 (pdf).--ISBN 978-1-4271-7789-6 (html)

     1. English language--Suffixes and prefixes--Juvenile literature.
I. Title.

PE1175.J64 2015   j428.1   C2014-907799-8
                                         C2014-907800-5

Library of Congress Cataloging-in-Publication Data

Johnson, Robin (Robin R.)
 The Word Wizard's book of prefixes and suffixes / Robin Johnson.
     pages cm. -- (Word Wizard)
 Includes index.
 ISBN 978-0-7787-1921-2 (reinforced library binding) --
ISBN 978-0-7787-1925-0 (pbk.) -- ISBN 978-1-4271-7793-3 (electronic pdf) --
ISBN 978-1-4271-7789-6 (electronic html)
1. English language--Suffixes and prefixes--Juvenile literature. 2. English
language--Parts of speech--Juvenile literature. 3. English language--
Grammar--Juvenile literature. 4. Language arts (Primary) 5. Language arts
(Elementary) I. Title. II. Title: Book of prefixes and suffixes.

 PE1175.J65 2015
 425'.92--dc23

                                         2014045068

Crabtree Publishing Company

Printed in Canada/022015/IH20141209

www.crabtreebooks.com   1-800-387-7650

Published in Canada
Crabtree Publishing
616 Welland Ave.
St. Catharines, Ontario
L2M 5V6

Published in the United States
Crabtree Publishing
PMB 59051
350 Fifth Avenue, 59th Floor
New York, New York 10118

Published in the United Kingdom
Crabtree Publishing
Maritime House
Basin Road North, Hove
BN41 1WR

Published in Australia
Crabtree Publishing
3 Charles Street
Coburg North
VIC 3058

Contents

Wonderful words

Words are magical! They can make you disappear. They help you unlock treasures. They let you fly like superheroes. Words are helpful. They transport you to faraway lands. Then they return you home again. Words are useful. They let you ask questions and uncover answers. They help you unwrap secrets and retell stories. Words are wonderful!

Beginnings and endings

Stories have magical beginnings and endings. They can start once upon a time. They can end happily ever after. Some words have magical beginnings and endings, too! They start with word parts called **prefixes**. They end with word parts called **suffixes**. Will you help the Word Wizards discover these magic words?

Words keep you undercover!

Words let you reach for the sky!

5

Root words

Did you know that words are like plants? They have roots and can grow! **Root words** are the main parts of words. They carry the basic meaning and can stand alone. The words "grow" and "plant" are root words. They do not have prefixes or suffixes added to them.

This flower has roots. Words have roots, too!

We find flowers in fields and gardens. We find root words everywhere!

Words grow

Words grow when we add prefixes and suffixes to them. The word "regrow" has the prefix "re." The word "plants" has the suffix "s." Learning how to add parts to root words helps your **vocabulary** grow. Your vocabulary is all the words you know and use.

Flowers grow when we water them. Words grow when we add prefixes and suffixes to them.

What is a prefix?

A prefix is a letter or group of letters added to the beginning of a word. We add prefixes to change the meaning of words. Like words, each prefix has a meaning. The prefix "pre" means "before." The word "fix" means "to join." We can add "pre" to "fix" to make the word "prefix." The new word means to join something in front of something else. That is what we do with prefixes!

These children go to preschool. They are too young for kindergarten.

Word Wizard in training

The Word Wizard needs your help to finish some **sentences**! Sentences are complete thoughts or ideas. Read the sentences below. They are missing some words. Point to a word on the list to fill in each blank. They all begin with the prefix "re." "Re" means "again." When you are finished, reread the sentences. The word "reread" means to read again.

recycle
rebuild
repay
retell
rewrite
reuse

Oh no! The dog ate my homework! Now I need to _____ it.

These boys are building a block tower. If it falls down, they will _____ it.

Changing the meaning

Some prefixes completely change the meaning of words. They make words that are the **opposite** of the root words. The prefixes "un" and "dis" both mean "not." The prefix "un" makes a happy girl unhappy. It lets you unlock a locked door. The prefix "dis" makes your little brother disagree with you. It makes ice cream quickly disappear!

Do you think these kids agree or disagree?

Is the boy lucky or unlucky? Is the ice cream appearing or disappearing?

Word Wizard
in training

Help the Word Wizard match up the words below. Some are root words. Others have prefixes. Use your finger to join words with opposite meanings. Can you discover all the answers?

clean   unable
like   dishonest
able   unclean
obey   unpack
pack   disobey
honest   dislike

Does this girl like or dislike jam?
Is her face clean or unclean?

What is a suffix?

A suffix is a letter or group of letters added to the end of a word. We add suffixes to change the meaning of words. We say, "A clown's unicycle has only one wheel. It is much easier to ride with training wheels!" The suffix "s" changes the meaning of the word "wheel." It changes it from **singular** to **plural**. Singular means only one. Plural means more than one.

Plural nouns

We add the suffix "s" to **nouns**. Nouns name people, animals, places, things, or ideas. Some nouns have special rules. We must add the suffix "es" to make them plural. The chart shows which nouns follow this rule.

Nouns end in	Singular nouns	Plural nouns
ch	lunch, watch	lunches, watches
sh	dish, crash	dishes, crashes
s	bus, cactus	buses, cactuses
ss	dress, glass	dresses, glasses
x	prefix, suffix	prefixes, suffixes
z	buzz, quiz	buzzes, quizzes

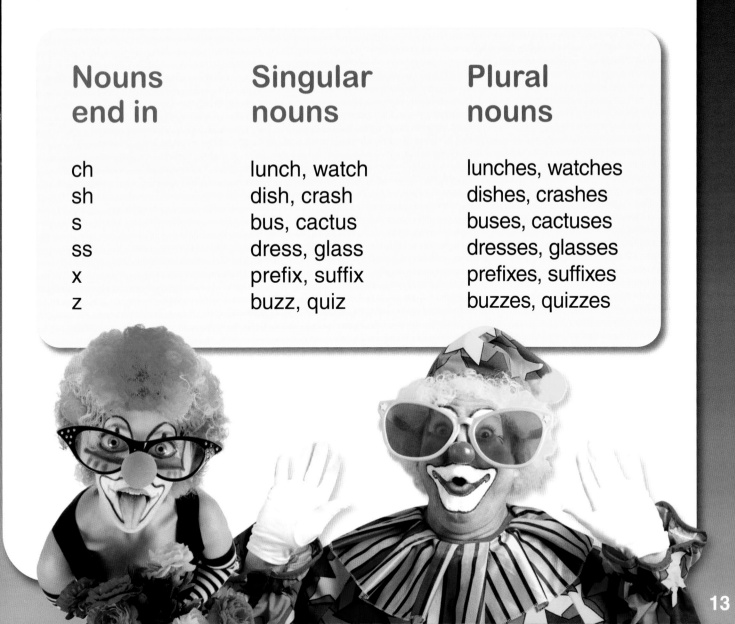

Time for tenses

Some suffixes tell us when things take place. We add these suffixes to **verbs**. Verbs are action words. The suffixes "s" and "ing" show action in the **present tense**. That means it is taking place right now. We say, "The girl jumps up and down. She is skipping rope." The verbs "jumps" and "skipping" are in the present tense.

We add the suffix "ed" to show actions in the **past tense**. Past tense means they have already taken place. We say, "The boy screamed when the frog hopped onto his nose." The verbs "screamed" and "hopped" are in the past tense.

Root rules

Some root words have special rules. We must change the words when we add suffixes to them. This chart shows some of the rules.

Types of root words	Rules	Root words + suffixes	New words
Root word ends in a silent "e"	Drop the "e" before adding a suffix that begins with a **vowel**	bake + ing dance + ing smile + ed use + ed	baking dancing smiled used
Root word ends in a "y" and has a **consonant** before the "y"	Change the "y" to an "i" except when adding "ing"	fly + ing hurry + ing carry + ed try + ed	flying hurrying carried tried
Root word ends in a single consonant and has a single vowel before the last letter	Double the consonant before adding a suffix that begins with a vowel	begin + ing run + ing plan + ed shop + ed	beginning running planned shopped

With or without

Some suffixes tell how much of something there is. The suffix "less" means "without." It tells us someone or something does not have any. If you are fearless, you have no fear. A fearless superhero is not afraid of anything! If something is spotless, it has no dirty spots. Not even a superhero could make it cleaner!

These fearless superheroes will save the world!

Full house

The suffix "ful" means "full of." It tells us someone or something has plenty. If you are hopeful, you have a lot of hope. If something is beautiful, it is full of beauty. The word "beauty" ends in the letter "y." Remember that we change the "y" to an "i" before we add a suffix.

This colorful dog has spots—even when it is spotless!

This beautiful girl was hopeful she would get a kitten.

I think I can

The suffix "able" means "able to be." We add it to words to show something can be done. We say, "The boy loves his teddy bear! It is huggable and lovable." The word "huggable" means good for hugging. We double the letter "g" because the suffix begins with a vowel. The word "lovable" means easy to love. We drop the silent "e" from "love" before we add the suffix.

The boy's teddy is unbearably huggable!

This girl wants to teach her friends a lesson. Are they teachable?

Word Wizard
in training

The Word Wizard is unable to finish the sentences below. Are you able to help her? Point to a word from the list to fill in each blank. When the sentences are readable, read them out loud.

enjoyable   movable
washable   valuable
eatable   closable

This boy stuffed everything into his suitcase—even himself! Now it is not _____.

These girls are taking a trip. Luckily their heavy suitcase is still _____!

Break it down

Some words have prefixes and suffixes. They look big and hard to understand! We can break them down to find their meanings. Look at the word "unbreakable." The root word is "break." The prefix "un" means "not." The suffix "able" means it can be done. So the word "unbreakable" describes something you cannot break.

This boy wants to open his piggy bank. Is it breakable or unbreakable?

Word Wizard in training

Help the Word Wizard break down some words. Read the sentences below. Study the red words in the sentences. What are the root words? What do the prefixes and suffixes mean? Then what do the whole words mean? Tell the Word Wizard how you discovered their meanings!

This girl is putting on a puppet show. She is *retelling* a story she heard in school.

These boys squeezed into a small box. Now they are crowded and *uncomfortable*!

Grow your own words

Now it is your turn to be a Word Wizard! Get a piece of paper and a pencil. Choose a root word from the chart. Write it down. Add a prefix or suffix to it. You changed the word like magic!

Rewrite the same root word. Add a different prefix or suffix to it. Then retry it with a new root word. Choose one from the list. Or think of your own. You can make lots of magic words. You are remarkable! You are unstoppable! You are a Word Wizard!

Magic words let you do unbelievable things!

22

Learning more

Books

-Ful and -Less, -Er and -Ness: What Is a Suffix? (Words Are CATegorical) by Brian P. Cleary. Millbrook Press Trade, 2014.

If You Were a Prefix (Word Fun) by Marcie Aboff. Picture Window Books, 2008.

If You Were a Suffix (Word Fun) by Marcie Aboff. Picture Window Books, 2008.

Pit Stop Prefixes (Grammar All-Stars) by Michael Ruscoe. Gareth Stevens Publishing, 2009.

Pre- and Re-, Mis- and Dis-: What Is a Prefix? (Words Are CATegorical) by Brian P. Cleary. Millbrook Press, 2013.

Soccer Goal Suffixes (Grammar All-Stars) by Michael Ruscoe. Gareth Stevens Publishing, 2009.

Websites

Play shooting, matching, and other prefix games at this great website.
www.turtlediary.com/grade-2-games/ela-games/prefix.html

Visit this super site for all sorts of suffix games.
www.turtlediary.com/grade-2-games/ela-games/suffix.html

Catch root words for prefix and suffix baskets in this fishy game.
www.ezschool.com/games/english/prefixsuffix/prefixsuffix.html

Choose prefixes and suffixes to make new words in this fun game.
www.funenglishgames.com/grammargames/prefixsuffix.html

Words to know

consonant (KON-suh-nuhnt) A letter of the alphabet that is not a vowel

noun (noun) A word that names a person, animal, place, thing, or idea

opposite (OP-uh-sit) Totally different

past tense (past tens) The verb form used to describe actions that have already taken place

plural (PLOO R-uh l) More than one

prefix (PREE-fiks) One or more letters added to the beginning of a word to change its meaning

present tense (PREZ-uhnt tens) The verb form used to describe actions taking place right now

root word (root wurd) The main part of a word that carries the basic meaning and can stand alone

sentence (SEN-tns) A complete thought or idea

singular (SING-gyuh-ler) Only one

suffix (SUHF-iks) One or more letters added to the end of a word to change its meaning

verb (vurb) An action word that tells what a person or thing is doing

vocabulary (voh-KAB-yuh-ler-ee) All the words a person knows and uses

vowel (VOU-uhl) The alphabet letters a, e, i, o, u, and sometimes y

Index